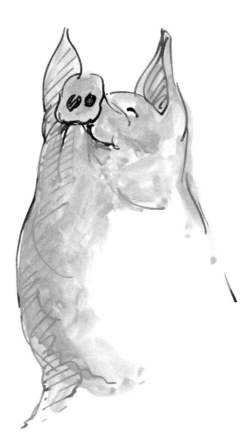

For the Youngs:
Please enjoy this and I
hope to see
you again.

Dave Page
12/29/94

VOICES · IN · POETRY

MARIANNE
MOORE

TEXT BY
DAVE PAGE

ILLUSTRATIONS BY
TOMI UNGERER

CREATIVE EDUCATION

*D*azzled, speechless—an alchemist without imple-
ments—one thinks of poetry as divine fire, a perquisite
of the gods. When under the spell of admiration or grat-
itude, I have hazarded a line, it never occurred to me
that anyone might think I imagined myself a poet. As
said previously, if what I write is called poetry it is
because there is no other category in which to put it.

From *Tell Me, Tell Me*

*W*hile a college student at Bryn Mawr in the early 1900s, Marianne Moore purchased a black tricorn hat, the kind worn by soldiers during the American Revolution. The hat became a fixture in her wardrobe. In pictures taken sixty years later—showing Moore smiling up from the cover of *Esquire* magazine, throwing out the first baseball on opening day at Yankee Stadium, or signing autographs with Muhammad Ali—the hat perches atop a braid of gray hair.

The trademark tricorn not only made Moore in-stantly recognizable but also earned her a reputation as an eccentric. Her originality, she claimed, was simply "a byproduct of sincerity," and uniqueness certainly shim-mered through her writing. Moore's ability to sense and record relationships between objects that at first seem unrelated, such as the "turkey foot" atop a pine tree, is unparalleled. In her work, readers will discover images that are, in the words of one critic, "difficult, intelligent, scrupulously accurate," and—like her hat—"charmingly whimsical."

Marianne Moore.

POETRY

I, too, dislike it: there are things that are

    important beyond all this fiddle.

Reading it, however, with a perfect contempt for it,

    one discovers in

it after all, a place for the genuine.

    Hands that can grasp, eyes

    that can dilate, hair that can rise

        if it must, these things are important not

    because a

high-sounding interpretation can be put upon them

    but because they are

useful. When they become so derivative as to become

    unintelligible,

the same thing may be said for all of us, that we

    do not admire what

    we cannot understand: the bat

        holding on upside down or in quest of

    something to

(continued)

eat, elephants pushing, a wild horse taking a roll, a

 tireless wolf under

 a tree, the immovable critic twitching his skin like

 a horse that feels a flea, the base-

 ball fan, the statistician—

 nor is it valid

 to discriminate against "business documents and

school-books"; all these phenomena are important. One

 must make a distinction

 however: when dragged into prominence by half

 poets, the result is not poetry,

nor till the poets among us can be

 "literalists of

 the imagination"—above

 insolence and triviality and can present

for inspection, imaginary gardens with real toads in them,

 shall we have

 it. In the meantime, if you demand on the one hand,

 the raw material of poetry in

 all its rawness and

 that which is on the other hand

 genuine, then you are interested in poetry.

From *Selected Poems*

C H I L D H O O D

*M*arianne Craig Moore never knew her father. Before she was born, John Moore suffered a mental breakdown following a failed business venture and was sent to an asylum in Massachusetts. His wife, Mary, took their one-year-old son to her father's home in Kirkwood, a suburb of St. Louis, where she gave birth to Marianne on November 15, 1887. Even after her husband's eventual recovery, Mary refused to reconcile with him or accept help from his family.

Despite the family breakup, Marianne's early years were peaceful ones. She lived contentedly with her mother, brother, and grandfather, a Presbyterian minister named John Riddle Warner. The Reverend Warner, a widower since 1863, cherished having his grandchildren in his home and wrote that those years were the happiest of his life. The two children returned their grandfather's love, and the affectionate pastor easily became the father they never had.

Throughout her childhood and for most of her life, Marianne's best friend was her brother. He was named John after his father, but everyone called him Warner. Together, he and Marianne leafed through picture books of birds in the parlor or lay awake at night inventing stories. They never fought or exchanged insults, and when Warner broke his arm, his five-year-old sister did everything for him—she even tied his shoes.

St. Louis, 1880.

You've seen a strawberry
that's had a struggle; yet
was, where the fragments met,

a hedgehog or a star-
fish for the multitude
of seeds. What better food

than apple seeds—the fruit
within the fruit—locked in
like counter-curved twin

hazelnuts? Frost that kills
the little rubber-plant-
leaves of *kok-saghyz*-stalks, can't

harm the roots; they still grow
in frozen ground. Once where
there was a prickly-pear-

leaf clinging to barbed wire,
a root shot down to grow

in earth two feet below;

as carrots form mandrakes
or a ram's-horn root some-
times. Victory won't come

to me unless I go
to it; a grape tendril
ties a knot in knots till

knotted thirty times—so
the bound twig that's under-
gone and over-gone, can't stir.

The weak overcomes its
menace, the strong over-
comes itself. What is there

like fortitude! What sap
went through that little thread
to make the cherry red!

From the collection *Nevertheless*

When Marianne was seven, her tranquil childhood was disrupted by the death of her grandfather. Unable to remain at the parsonage, Mary Moore traveled east with her two children and moved in with her brother near Pittsburgh. Marianne first began to try her hand at poetry during this time, and her mother included a few of her rhymes in a letter to relatives in 1895: "Pussy in the cradle lies—and sweetly dreams of gnats and flies."

The subject of Marianne's first verse is not surprising, as she shared a love of animals with the rest of her family. The Warner parsonage had been home to kittens, puppies, and even a pet alligator, Tibby, whom Marianne said she tended "as if he were a little deity." Later, even the family's letters contained many references to animals. Mrs. Moore often called Warner by the name "Toady" and signed herself as "Turtle." Marianne used "Dear Fish" as a salutation and ended her letters with the name "Fangs." After the publication of *The Wind in the Willows* in 1908, Mrs. Moore was frequently called "Mole," Marianne assumed the name "Rat," and Warner took "Badger."

Marianne grew to admire the independence and endurance of animals and later used them as symbols in her poetry. Armored animals, in particular, such as the anteaterlike creature of "The Pangolin" and the mythical monster of "O to be a Dragon," earned a privileged spot in her poetic zoo.

An illustration by Ernest H. Shepard from The Wind in the Willows.

O TO BE A DRAGON

*I*f I, like Solomon, . . .

could have my wish—

my wish . . . O to be a dragon,

a symbol of the power of Heaven—of silkworm

size or immense; at times invisible.

Felicitous phenomenon!

From the collection *O to be a Dragon*

*I*f there was one constant in Marianne's life, it was her mother's devotion to learning. Mary Moore had graduated from college at a time when few women pursued higher education, and she was determined that her children follow the same path. To that end, she took them on educational field trips and encouraged them to take advantage of the public library and local lecture hall of Carlisle, Pennsylvania, where they had moved in 1896. And, despite what she called the "extravagance," she sent them to private schools.

These exertions to prepare Marianne for college were not particularly successful, however, and Mary Moore once complained that her youngest child "was not an especially adept pupil." During the summer of 1905, a family friend had to help Marianne prepare for the strenuous entrance examination at Bryn Mawr. The tutoring paid off when Marianne managed to gain acceptance to the exclusive college outside Philadelphia.

Marianne was very homesick during her first days at Bryn Mawr. After failing German and Italian, she thought about leaving school. Her one refuge was drawing. She had won prizes for her art in Carlisle and now began to spend hours in the college's biology laboratory, sketching exacting pictures of birds and flowers. The disinterested passion of the sciences appealed to her, and she considered studying medicine—especially since her skills with languages seemed limited.

It wasn't that she disliked English; on the contrary, she loved to read and write. But her instructors felt that her thinking was not logical enough for the development of understandable essays. Admittedly, she did tend to write in unusual ways. In fact, one of her papers contained only a series of quotes. "When a thing has been said so well that it could not be said better," she asked, "why paraphrase it?" In the future, Marianne would use a similar type of logic in her best poems.

In spite of some of the faculty's unsympathetic reactions to her literary efforts, Marianne continued to set down what she later recognized as "prettified and romantic imitations" of European writers. She was not alone in her endeavors, since writing was taken very seriously at Bryn Mawr. Eventually, a friend of Marianne's who was an editor on the school's literary magazine asked her to submit a few of her pieces, and several of these appeared in the *Tipyn O'Bob*. Although responses to her stories were mixed, in the spring of 1907, Marianne herself was elected to the editorial board of the "Typ."

As Marianne became more involved in college life, she gained many friends and developed wide-ranging interests, including feminism and social reform. It was during this period of awakening that Marianne first saw, admired, and purchased a black tricorn hat—one more symbol for the woman who would develop, according to biographer Charles Molesworth, into "a poet of tokens and emblems and rare objects."

A basketball game at Bryn Mawr in the early 1900s.

VALUES IN USE

I attended school and I liked the place—
grass and little locust-leaf shadows like lace.

Writing was discussed. They said, "We create
values in the process of living, daren't await

their historic progress." Be abstract
and you'll wish you'd been specific; it's a fact.

What was I studying? Values in use,
"judged on their own ground." Am I still abstruse?

Walking along, a student said offhand,
"'Relevant' and 'plausible' were words I understand."

A pleasing statement, anonymous friend.
Certainly the means must not defeat the end.

From *O to be a Dragon*

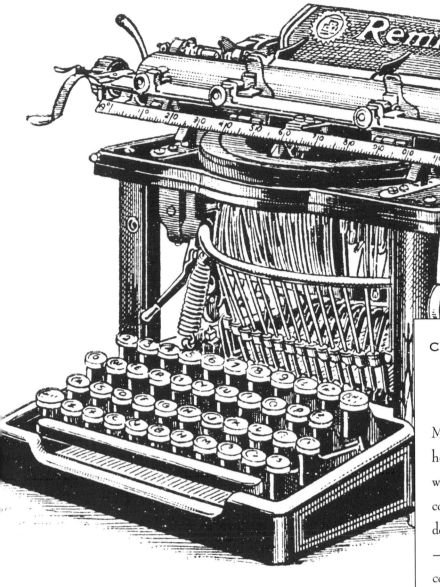

$\mathcal{M}$oore's forays into the pages of Bryn Mawr's "Typ" had made her comfortable thinking about herself as a writer, but after graduating from college she was not sure where or how to let her talents mature. She considered going to art school or getting a job, but with a degree in history and politics—fields open to few women—her opportunities were limited. When a Bryn Mawr counselor suggested she learn to type and take short-hand, Moore resigned herself to returning home and taking courses at Carlisle Commercial College.

She first used her new secretarial skills during the summer of 1910 at a school in Lake Placid, New York, run by Melvil Dewey, the man who developed the decimal classification system used by libraries. Moore's duties consisted of proofreading the publications Dewey sponsored and taking dictation from Dewey himself, but she also found time to walk in the woods and socialize. In August, she sent a letter to Warner telling him that she had seven suitors. By the end of the summer, she wrote again to say that she took none of the young men seriously. When a local matron tried to rekindle one of the flames, Moore complained that there was nothing more odious in modern society than a matchmaker. It was one of the last references she ever made to matrimony.

MARRIAGE
Lines 1–20

*T*his institution,

perhaps one should say enterprise

out of respect for which

one says one need not change one's mind

about a thing one has believed in,

requiring public promises

of one's intention

to fulfil a private obligation:

I wonder what Adam and Eve

think of it by this time,

this fire-gilt steel

alive with goldenness;

how bright it shows—

"of circular traditions and impostures,

committing many spoils,"

requiring all one's criminal ingenuity

to avoid!

Psychology which explains everything

explains nothing,

and we are still in doubt.

From *Selected Poems*

At the age of twenty-three, Moore began work at the United States Indian School in Carlisle. Richard Pratt, a former cavalryman who had ridden with Custer, started the school in an abandoned army barracks on the outskirts of town. Moore spent several years there teaching such subjects as typing and commercial English. One of her first students, Jim Thorpe, went on to dominate the 1912 Olympic Games by winning both the decathlon and pentathlon. She thought her star pupil "chivalrous and kind," but she did not think as highly of her own teaching skills. Moore told interviewers she had been a poor instructor and "would have preferred to remain home and read."

During her four years at the Indian School, Moore finally tasted her first publishing success outside Bryn Mawr. One of her classmates, Hilda Doolittle (H. D.), had married the publisher of an English literary magazine called *The Egoist*. She asked her husband to look at Moore's poems; he then printed two in the May 1915 issue, including "To the Soul of Progress" (later titled "To Military Progress"). A month later, Chicago-based *Poetry* magazine also featured several of Moore's poems.

These appearances brought Moore recognition from renowned poet Ezra Pound, who insisted that she and a few others were the most important voices among the newest generation of poets.

The 1907 Carlisle Indian football team. Jim Thorpe is in the top row, second from left.

You use your mind

like a millstone to grind

    chaff.

You polish it

and with your warped wit

    laugh

At your torso,

prostrate where the crow

    falls

on such faint hearts

as its god imparts,

    calls

and claps its wings

till the tumult brings

    more

black minute-men

to revive again,

    war

at little cost.

They cry for the lost

    head

and seek their prize

till the evening sky's

    red.

From *Selected Poems*

*I*n 1916 Marianne and her mother moved from Carlisle to live with Warner, who had been called to be a pastor of a church in Chatham, New Jersey. Mary Moore was very pleased to resume the family triangle—too much so, perhaps. Overprotective and manipulative, she tried to control her children, and neither Marianne nor Warner resisted. She even discouraged Warner from marrying and suggested that his sister would be better suited to life in a parsonage because she did not seem to need "supportive love" like other women. Indeed, at twenty-nine Marianne seemed quite content to go back to her childhood living arrangements.

Despite Mary Moore's efforts, however, the family dynamic quickly changed. With war spreading across Europe, Warner began to spend more and more of his time with the militia unit he had joined. By 1917 he had earned a Navy commission and resigned his ministry at Chatham. Life at sea gave him new confidence. Ignoring his mother's disapproval, he married Constance Eustis after a brief courtship. Warner's defection from the family triangle, excused in part by wartime circumstances, caused great pain for Mary Moore, who refused to mention her new daughter-in-law in letters to Warner.

Although Warner's escape caused dissension in the family, it also provided Marianne with an opportunity for professional growth. Now that they could no longer live in the parsonage, she and her mother took an apartment in Greenwich Village in Manhattan, the heart of literary modernism. Although Marianne had earlier told her brother that she had no desire to live in New York City, she soon wrote, "I like New York, the little quiet part of it in which my mother and I live. I like to see the tops of the masts from our door and go to the wharf and look at the craft on the river."

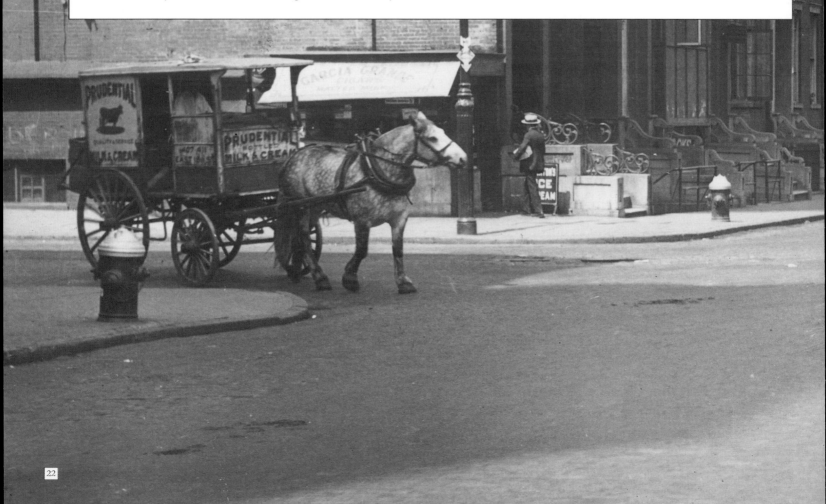

Greenwich Village in the late 1920s.

Make a fuss
and be tedious.

I'm annoyed?
yes; am—avoid

"adore"
and "bore";

am, I
say, by

the word
bore, bored;

refuse
to use

"divine"
to mean

something
pleasing;

"terrific color"
for some horror.

Though flat,
myself, I'd say that

"Atlas"
(pressed glass)

looks best
embossed.

I refuse
to use

"enchant,"
"dement";

even "fright-
ful plight"
(however justified)

or "frivol-
ous fool"
(however suitable).

I've escaped?
am still trapped

by these
word diseases.

No pauses—
the phrases

lack lyric
force; sound capric-

like Attic
capric-Alcaic,

or freak
calico-Greek.

(Not verse
of course)
I'm sure of this:

Nothing mundane is divine;
Nothing divine is mundane.

From *The Complete Poems of Marianne Moore*

*H*aving earned a reputation as a promising new poet, Moore socialized in New York City with a circle of significant contemporaries, such as poets William Carlos Williams and Wallace Stevens. Publisher and poet Alfred Kreymborg remembered that Moore's "mellifluous flow of polysyllables . . . held every man in awe" at their New York get-togethers. At one party, another guest was so smitten by her presentation of "England" that he urged her to submit the poem to *The Dial*, one of the most highly regarded American magazines of the 1920s. Moore replied that she already had and that it had been rejected. Her admirer turned out to be Scofield Thayer, one of the owners of *The Dial*. He asked her to resubmit. Eventually two of her poems were published in the April 1920 issue, making her the first of her group to gain such a prestigious outlet.

A year later, Moore's college friend, H. D., contacted her from England to ask if she and some colleagues could publish in book form twenty-four of Marianne's poems that had previously appeared in magazines. Moore consented, and 300 copies of the slim softcover edition, simply entitled *Poems*, hit English bookstores in July 1921. Both Moore and her mother worried that the poems were not yet polished enough to be collected, but the reception for her first volume was good. One of the biggest boosts came from T. S. Eliot. Born in St. Louis ten months after Moore, he was already considered a leading figure in modern poetry. His essay on *Poems* commented on Moore's peculiar and brilliant use of "the curious jargon produced in America by universal university education."

William Carlos Williams.

T. S. Eliot.

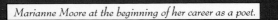

Marianne Moore at the beginning of her career as a poet.

With its baby rivers and little towns, each with its
   abbey or its cathedral,
with voices—one voice perhaps, echoing through
   the transept—the
criterion of suitability and convenience: and Italy
with its equal shores—contriving an epicureanism
from which the grossness has been extracted,

and Greece with its goat and its gourds,
the nest of modified illusions: and France,
the "chrysalis of the nocturnal butterfly,"
in whose products mystery of construction
diverts one from what was originally one's object—
substance at the core: and the East with its snails, its
   emotional

shorthand and jade cockroaches, its rock crystal and
   its imperturbability,
all of museum quality: and America where there
is the little old ramshackle victoria in the south,
where cigars are smoked on the street in the north;
where there are no proofreaders, no silkworms,
   no digressions;

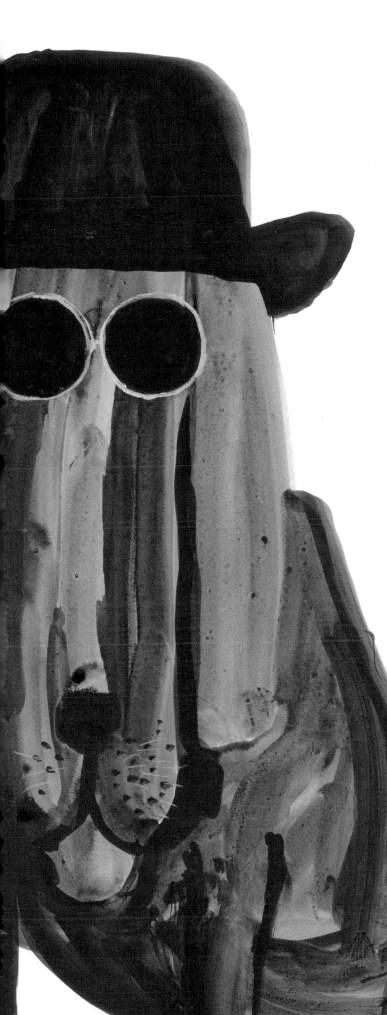

the wild man's land; grassless, linksless, languageless

country in which letters are written

not in Spanish, not in Greek, not in Latin, not in

shorthand,

but in plain American which cats and dogs can read!

The letter *a* in psalm and calm when

pronounced with the sound of *a* in candle, is very

noticeable, but

why should continents of misapprehension

have to be accounted for by the fact?

(continued)

Does it follow that because there are poisonous toadstools

which resemble mushrooms, both are dangerous?

Of mettlesomeness which may be mistaken for appetite,

of heat which may appear to be haste,

no conclusions may be drawn.

To have misapprehended the matter is to have confessed

that one has not looked far enough.

The sublimated wisdom of China, Egyptian discernment,

the cataclysmic torrent of emotion

compressed in the verbs of the Hebrew language,

the books of the man who is able to say,

"I envy nobody but him, and him only,

who catches more fish than

I do"—the flower and fruit of all that noted superiority—

if not stumbled upon in America,

must one imagine that it is not there?

It has never been confined to one locality.

From *Selected Poems*

THE DIAL

SEPTEMBER 1928

EDITOR

In 1924 Moore's career took a leap forward with the publication of her second book, *Observations*. Later that year, she won a $2,000 prize for achievement in poetry sponsored by the founders of *The Dial*. Within another year, Scofield Thayer appointed her acting director of the magazine. His move surprised no one, especially since his friends knew that Thayer had more than just a professional interest in Marianne. The two always maintained a formal attitude, however, and there is no hint in their correspondence that their relationship ever developed along romantic lines.

Soon after she began her duties at *The Dial*, Thayer resigned and Moore took over the day-to-day management of the journal. The honor of such an important position was tempered by drawbacks. Not only did her responsibilities as editor keep her from writing, but she also had to reject submissions from poets who were only trying—as she had—to make a name for themselves, or, worse yet, were her friends.

Despite these difficulties, Moore maintained the high standards of the magazine. Her comments on American literature in the pages of *The Dial* over the four years she worked there established a good number of literary reputations for the next several decades.

There is a great amount of poetry in unconscious

fastidiousness. Certain Ming

products, imperial floor coverings of coach-

wheel yellow, are well enough in their way but I

have seen something

that I like better—a

mere childish attempt to make an

imperfectly bal-

lasted animal stand up,

similar determination to make a pup

eat his meat from the plate.

I remember a swan under the willows in Oxford,

with flamingo-colored, maple-

leaflike feet. It reconnoitered like a battle-

ship. Disbelief and conscious fastidiousness were

ingredients in its

disinclination to move. Finally its hardihood was

not proof against its

proclivity to more fully appraise such bits

of food as the stream

bore counter to it; it made away with what I gave it

to eat. I have seen this swan and

I have seen you; I have seen ambition without

understanding in a variety of forms. Happening

to stand by an ant-hill, I have

seen a fastidious ant carrying a stick north,

south, east, west, till it turned on

itself, struck out from the flower bed into

the lawn,

and returned to the point

from which it had started. Then abandoning the stick as

useless and overtaxing its

jaws with a particle of whitewash—pill-like but

heavy—it again went through the same course of

procedure.

What is

there in being able

to say that one has dominated the stream in

an attitude of self-defense;

in proving that one has had the experience

of carrying a stick?

From *Selected Poems*

33

C H A N G E S

*P*erhaps as a harbinger of the country's coming financial crisis, *The Dial* closed its doors by mid-1929. To compensate for the loss of income, the forty-one-year-old poet took a job in a library. Two months later, Moore resigned and moved across the East River to Brooklyn so that she and her mother could be closer to Warner, who had been transferred to the Navy Yard there. Moore enjoyed Brooklyn and resumed writing poetry. In 1935 she won the Ernest Hartsock Memorial Prize for her book *Poems*.

For the next dozen years, Moore continued to publish highly regarded poems. Then, in July 1947, her string of successes was interrupted by the death of her mother, who succumbed to illness at the age of eighty-five. The loss of her strong-willed mother deeply affected Moore. On the surface, she acted with a quiet resolve and insisted she would not compromise her art by using her writing as "a source of moral strength." Yet three weeks later, she began a poem that was obviously about her mother. Leaving the piece unfinished, she tried to refocus her energies by working on translations of some French fables. When these were rejected by a publisher the following year, she wrote to her brother about her grief and weakness. She took to her bed for weeks at a time and contemplated seeing a psychiatrist.

Due to the kind attention of friends and admirers, within a couple of years Moore recovered sufficiently to begin work on another book of poetry. With the publication of *Collected Poems* in 1951, Moore finally gained a modicum of fame outside the literary world. In 1952 she won the National Book Award and the Pulitzer Prize; in 1953 she won the Bollingen Prize in Poetry. *Newsweek* magazine ran a small photograph of her alongside a large picture of her former student Jim Thorpe, who had just been named outstanding athlete of the first half of the twentieth century. "The Tonight Show" featured Moore as a guest, and *Life* magazine went on a photo tour of a zoo with her. "The animal is an exemplar of art because of his naturalness," she insisted. "His self-discipline provides a useful lesson for errant man."

Marianne Moore and Langston Hughes (right) at a Long Island University poetry festival, 1952.

*W*inked too much and were afraid of snakes. The
zebras, supreme in
their abnormality; the elephants with their fog-colored
skin
and strictly practical appendages
were there, the small cats; and the parakeet—
trivial and humdrum on examination, destroying
bark and portions of the food it could not eat.

I recall their magnificence, now not more magnificent
than it is dim. It is difficult to recall the ornament,
speech, and precise manner of what one might
call the minor acquaintances twenty
years back; but I shall not forget him—that
Gilgamesh among
the hairy carnivora—that cat with the

wedge-shaped, slate-gray marks on its forelegs and the
resolute tail,
astringently remarking, "They have imposed on us
with their pale
half-fledged protestations, trembling about
in inarticulate frenzy, saying
it is not for us to understand art; finding it
all so difficult, examining the thing

as if it were inconceivably arcanic, as symmet-
rically frigid as if it had been carved out of chrysoprase
or marble—strict with tension, malignant
in its power over us and deeper
than the sea when it proffers flattery in exchange
for hemp,
rye, flax, horses, platinum, timber, and fur."

From *Selected Poems*

Ebbets Field, home of the Brooklyn Dodgers from 1913 to 1957.

*W*ell into her seventies, Moore bounced around the country as the poet in the tricorn hat, delighting those who came to listen to her verse. Strangely, her poetic reputation was most closely linked with baseball. As a beginning writer Moore had been attracted to the game's slang. She used phrases like "old gum glove" and "round-tripper" in letters to Warner. In an interview with *Harper's* several decades later, she said that baseball appealed to her because of its displays of "dexterity— with a logic of memory that makes strategy possible." Baseball was also good business. In the fall of 1956, her baseball poem "Hometown Piece for Messrs. Alston and Reese" appeared on the front page of the *New York Herald-Tribune* on the first day of the World Series. Overnight, more people read her work than all her previous audiences combined.

Although Moore championed her hometown Brooklyn Dodgers, she later supported the Yankees and Mets. The owner of the Yankees invited her and Warner to watch a game with the mayor of New York, John Lindsay. The owner of the Mets did likewise. Moore also wrote a poem about Casey Stengel, manager of the Yankees and later the Mets.

Moore soon discovered that her newfound recognition made her extremely popular as a party guest. Trying to oblige, she attended almost as many New York functions in the 1960s as she had in her youth. "Drat it! / Celebrity costs privacy!" she teased in a poem. Nevertheless, she rarely turned down an invitation and often welcomed visitors to her apartment for informal discussions on subjects as diverse as grocery stores, Shakespeare, and trumpet music.

To the tune:

"Li'l baby, don't say a word: Mama goin' to buy you

a mockingbird.

Bird don't sing: Mama goin' to sell it and buy a

brass ring."

"Millennium," yes; "pandemonium"!

Roy Campanella leaps high. Dodgerdom

crowned, had Johnny Podres on the mound.

Buzzie Bavasi and the Press gave ground;

the team slapped, mauled, and asked the Yankees'

match,

"How did you feel when Sandy Amoros made the

catch?"

"I said to myself"—pitcher for all innings—

"as I walked back to the mound I said, 'Everything's

getting better and better.'" (Zest: they've zest.

"'Hope springs eternal in the Brooklyn breast.'"

And would the Dodger Band in 8, row 1, relax

if they saw the collector of income tax?

Ready with a tune if that should occur:

"Why Not Take All of Me—All of Me, Sir?")

Another series. Round-tripper Duke at bat,

"Four hundred feet from home-plate"; more like that.

A-squat in double-headers four hundred times a day,
he says that in a measure the pleasure is the pay:

catcher to pitcher, a nice easy throw
almost as if he'd just told it to go.

Willie Mays should be a Dodger. He should—
a lad for Roger Craig and Clem Labine to elude;

but you have an omen, pennant-winning Peewee,
on which we are looking superstitiously.

Ralph Branca has Preacher Roe's number; recall?
and there's Don Bessent; he can really fire the ball.

As for Gil Hodges, in custody of first—
"He'll do it by himself." Now a specialist—versed

in an extension reach far into the box seats—
he lengthens up, leans and gloves the ball. He defeats

expectation by a whisker. The modest star,
irked by one misplay, is no hero by a hair;

in a strikeout slaughter when what could matter more,
he lines a homer to the signboard and has changed

the score.

(continued)

A neat bunt, please; a cloud-breaker, a drive
like Jim Gilliam's great big one. Hope's alive.

Homered, flied out, fouled? Our "stylish stout"
so nimble Campanella will have him out.

Then for his nineteenth season, a home run—

with four of six runs batted in—Carl Furillo's

      the big gun;

almost dehorned the foe—has fans dancing in delight.

Jake Pitler and his Playground "get a Night"—

Jake, that hearty man, made heartier by a harrier

who can bat as well as field—Don Demeter.

Shutting them out for nine innings—hitter too

Carl Erskine leaves Cimoli nothing to do.

Take off the goat-horns, Dodgers, that egret

which two very fine base-stealers can offset.

You've got plenty: Jackie Robinson

and Campy and big Newk, and Dodgerdom again

watching everything you do. You won last year.

      Come on.

From *Selected Poems*

M E M O R I A L

*I*n 1969 Marianne Moore suffered a stroke that forced her to stop writing. Correspondence was entrusted to Ethel Taylor, her secretary, who claimed that Moore felt no pain as she declined in health. On February 5, 1972, Moore died peacefully in her sleep while at her home on West Ninth Street in Manhattan. She was eighty-four.

The following day, *The New York Times* ran a full-page tribute to Moore and her work. Two memorial services were held at Lafayette Presbyterian, the Brooklyn church Moore had attended for many years. At another memorial service in Italy, Ezra Pound recited her poem "What Are Years?"

The poet often described as "The World's Greatest Living Observer" was gone, but her legacy remains.

Yankee Stadium, 1968: Marianne Moore gets ready to toss the first pitch on opening day.

WHAT ARE YEARS?

*W*hat is our innocence,

what is our guilt? All are

   naked, none is safe. And whence

is courage: the unanswered question,

the resolute doubt—

dumbly calling, deafly listening—that

is misfortune, even death,

     encourages others

     and in its defeat, stirs

   the soul to be strong? He

sees deep and is glad, who

   accedes to mortality

and in his imprisonment rises

upon himself as

the sea in a chasm, struggling to be

free and unable to be,

     in its surrendering

     finds its continuing.

   So he who strongly feels,

behaves. The very bird,

   grown taller as he sings, steels

his form straight up. Though he is captive,

his mighty singing

says, satisfaction is a lowly

thing, how pure a thing is joy.

     This is mortality,

     this is eternity.

From the collection *What Are Years?*

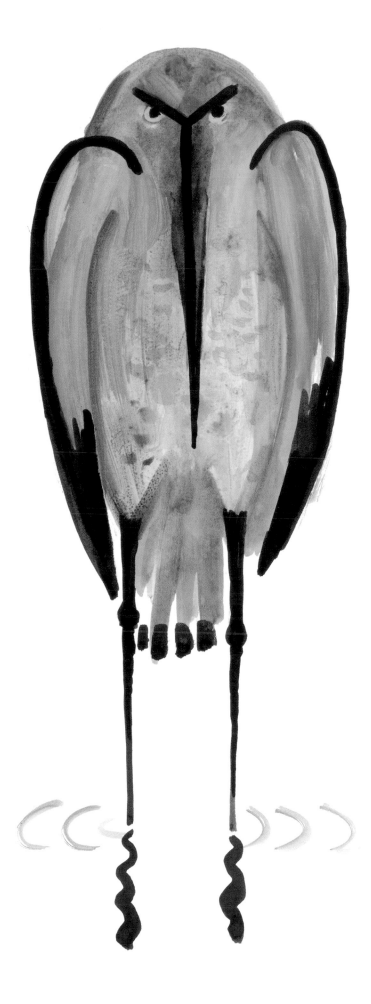

ACKNOWLEDGMENTS

Edited by S. L. Berry and Nancy Loewen
Photo research by Ann Schwab
Design assistant: Mindy Belter

PHOTO CREDITS

The Bettmann Archive
Culver Pictures, Inc.
The Everett Collection
FPG

New York Public Library
North Wind Picture Archives
Wide World Photos

Illustration from THE WIND IN THE WILLOWS: Reprinted with permission of
Charles Scribner's Sons, an imprint of Macmillan Publishing Company from THE WIND IN THE WILLOWS
by Kenneth Grahame, illustrated by Ernest H. Shepard. Copyright 1933, 1953
Charles Scribner's Sons; copyrights renewed © 1962 Ernest H. Shepard and
1981 Charles Scribner's Sons and Mary Eleanor Jessie Knox.

POETRY CREDITS

SELECTED WORKS BY MARIANNE MOORE

POETRY
Poems, 1921
Observations, 1924
Selected Poems, 1935
What Are Years? 1941
Nevertheless, 1944
Collected Poems, 1951
Predilections, 1955
Like a Bulwark, 1956
O To Be a Dragon, 1959
A Marianne Moore Reader, 1961
  (poetry and prose)

The Arctic Ox, 1964
*Tell Me, Tell Me: Granite, Steel, and
  Other Topics*, 1966
The Complete Poems of Marianne Moore,
  1967

TRANSLATIONS
The Fables of La Fontaine, 1954
Selected Fables of La Fontaine, 1955
*Puss in Boots, The Sleeping Beauty &
  Cinderella*, 1963

INDEX

Published by Creative Education
123 South Broad Street, Mankato, Minnesota 56001
Creative Education is an imprint of Creative Education, Inc.
Copyright © 1994 Creative Education, Inc.
International copyrights reserved in all countries.
No part of this book may be reproduced in any form without
written permission from the publisher.
Printed in Italy.
Art Direction: Rita Marshall
Designed by: Stephanie Blumenthal
Illustrations by Tomi Ungerer
Library of Congress Cataloging-in-Publication Data
Page, Dave.
    Marianne Moore / written by Dave Page.
        p.   cm. — (Voices in poetry)
    Includes bibliographical references and index.
    Summary: Examines the life of the American poet and
presents some of her poems.
    ISBN 0-88682-615-2
    1. Moore, Marianne, 1887–1972—Biography—Juvenile lit-
erature.   2. Poets, American—20th century—Biography—
Juvenile literature.   3. Young adult poetry, American. [1. Moore,
Marianne, 1887–1972. 2. Poets, American.   3. American
poetry.] I. Title.   II. Series: Voices in poetry (Mankato, Minn.)
PS3525.O5616Z73   1993
811'.52—dc20
[B]

93-3375
CIP
AC